Mobil New Zealand Nature Series
SEASHORE LIFE

Mobil New Zealand Nature Series
SEASHORE LIFE

R. K. Dell
Illustrated by Eric Heath

HEINEMANN REED

Published by Heinemann Reed, a division of Octopus
Publishing Group (NZ) Ltd, 39 Rawene Road, Birkenhead,
Auckland. Associated companies, branches and
representatives throughout the world.

This book is copyright. Except for the purpose of fair
reviewing, no part of this publication may be reproduced or
transmitted in any form or by any means, electronic or
mechanical, including photocopying, recording or any
information storage and retrieval system, without
permission in writing from the publisher. Infringers of
copyright render themselves liable to prosecution.

ISBN 0 7900 0151 9

© 1981, R.K. Dell and Eric Heath
First published 1981
Reprinted 1989

Printed in Singapore

CONTENTS

	Page	Plate
Introduction		1
Sea squirts (*Tunicates or Ascidians*)	15	1
1. Sea tulip (*Pyura pachydermatina*)	15	1
2. Transparent sea squirt (*Corella eumyota*)	15	1
3. Saddle sea squirt (*Cnemidiocarpa bicornuta*)	15	1
Sea urchins	17	2
4. Common sea urchin, sea egg or kina (*Evechinus chloroticus*)	17	2
5. Heart urchin (*Echinocardium cordatum*)	17	2
6. Cake urchin, sand dollar or snapper biscuit (*Fellaster zelandicus*)	17	2
Starfishes	19	3
7. Biscuit star (*Pentagonaster pulchellus*)	19	3
8. Cushion star (*Patiriella regularis*)	19	3
9. Reef Star (*Stichaster australis*)	19	3
Brittlestars	21	4
10. Mottled sand star (*Ophionereis fasciatus*)	21	4
11. Oar sand star (*Ophiopteris antipodum*)	21	4
Sea cucumber	21	4
12. Common sea cucumber (*Stichopus mollis*)	21	4
Chitons or coat and mail shells	23	5
13. Noble chiton (*Eudoxochiton nobilis*)	23	5
14. Snake's skin chiton (*Sypharochiton pelliserpentis*)	23	5
15. Butterfly chiton (*Cryptoconchus porosus*)	23	5
16. Variable chiton (*Ischnochiton maorianus*)	23	5
Squids, octopuses and their allies (*Cephalopoda*)	25	6
17. Common octopus (*Octopus maorum*)	25	6
18. Paper nautilus (*Argonauta nodosa*)	25	6
19. Broad-finned squid (*Sepioteuthis bilineata*)	27	7
20. Arrow squid (*Notodarus sloani*)	27	7
21. Jewelled squid (*Sepioloidea pacifica*)	27	7
22. Ram's horn squid (*Spirula spirula*)	27	7
Bivalves	29	8
23. Green edged mussel (*Perna canaliculus*)	29	8
24. Black edged mussel (*Mytilus edulis aoteanus*)	29	8
25. Horse mussel (*Atrina zelandica*)	29	8
26. Nesting mussel (*Modiolarca impacta*)	31	9
27. Ribbed mussel (*Aulacomya maorianus*)	31	9
28. Common scallop (*Pecten novaezelandiae*)	31	9
29. Fan scallop (*Chlamys zelandiae*)	31	9
30. Tuatua (*Paphies (Mesodesma) subtriangulatum*)	33	10

31. Pipi (*Paphies australis*)	33	10
32. Toheroa (*Paphies (Mesodesma) ventricosa*)	33	10
33. New Zealand or common cockle (*Austrovenus stutchburyi*)	33	10
34. Coarse dosinia (*Dosinia anus*)	35	11
35. Frilled Venus shell (*Bassina yatei*)	35	11
36. Morning star (*Tawera spissa*)	35	11
37. Rock borer (*Anchomas similis*)	35	11
38. Large wedge shell (*Macomona liliana*)	37	12
39. Triangle shell (*Spisula aequilateralis*)	37	12
40. Rock oyster (*Crassostrea glomerata*)	37	12
41. Dredge oyster or Stewart Island oyster (*Ostrea lutaria*)	37	12
Univalves	39	13
42. Paua (*Haliotis iris*)	39	13
43. Pink paua (*Haliotis australis*)	39	13
44. Shield shell (*Scutus breviculus*)	39	13
45. Ornate limpet (*Cellana ornata*)	41	14
46. Radiate limpet (*Cellana radians*)	41	14
47. Fragile limpet (*Atalacmea fragilis*)	41	14
48. Ribbed slipper limpet (*Maoricrypta costata*)	41	14
49. Cunningham's tiger shell (*Maurea selecta*)	43	15
50. Large tiger shell (*Maurea tigris*)	43	15
51. Opal top shell (*Cantharidus opalus*)	43	15
52. Black nerita (*Nerita melanotragus*)	43	15
53. Cook's turban shell (*Cookia sulcata*)	45	16
54. Circular saw shell (*Astraea heliotropium*)	45	16
55. Cat's eye (*Turbo smaragdus*)	45	16
56. Large periwinkle (*Littorina cincta*)	45	16
57. Large trumpet (*Charonia lampas capax*)	47	17
58. Helmet shell (*Xenophalium pyrum*)	47	17
59. Southern volute (*Alcithoe swainsoni*)	47	17
60. Southern olive (*Baryspira australis*)	47	17
61. Dark rock shell (*Haustrum haustorium*)	49	18
62. White rock shell (*Thais orbita*)	49	18
63. Oyster borer (*Lepsiella scobina*)	49	18
64. Large ostrich foot (*Struthiolaria papulosa*)	49	18
65. Knobbed whelk (*Austrofusus glans*)	51	19
66. Spotted whelk (*Cominella maculosa*)	51	19
67. Speckled whelk (*Cominella adspersa*)	51	19
68. Lined whelk (*Buccinulum powelli*)	51	19
69. Warty sea slug (*Archidoris wellingtonensis*)	53	20
70. Mud snail (*Amphibola crenata*)	53	20
71. Fragile bubble shell (*Haminoea zelandiae*)	53	20
72. Turret shell (*Maoricolpus roseus*)	53	20
Crustacea	55	21
73. Red rock crab (*Plagusia chabrus*)	55	21
74. Large shore crab (*Leptograpsus variegatus*)	55	21

75. Common rock crab (*Hemigrapsus edwardsi*) — 55, 21
76. Hairy seaweed crab (*Notomithrax ursus*) — 57, 22
77. Common swimming crab (*Ovalipes catharus*) — 57, 22
78. New Zealand cancer crab (*Cancer novaezelandiae*) — 57, 22
79. Common crayfish (*Jasus edwardsi*) — 59, 23
80. Smoothtail crayfish (*Jasus verreauxi*) — 59, 23
81. Common shrimp (*Palaemon affinis*) — 59, 23
82. Half crab (*Petrolisthes elongatus*) — 61, 24
83. Common hermit crab (*Pagurus novaezelandiae*) — 61, 24

Barnacles — 63, 25

84. Goose barnacle (*Lepas*) — 63, 25
85. Pink barnacle (*Balanus decorus*) — 63, 25
86. Modest barnacle (*Elminius modestus*) — 63, 25

Lamp shell — 65, 26

87. Large red lamp shell (*Magasella sanguinea*) — 65, 26

Jointed worms — 65, 26

88. Green sea centipede (*Perinereis novaehollandiae*) — 65, 26
89. Sea mouse (*Aphrodite australis*) — 65, 26

Jellyfish — 67, 27

90. Portuguese man-of-war or blue bottle (*Physalia physalis*) — 67, 27
91. Common jellyfish (*Aurelia aurata*) — 67, 27
92. By-the-wind sailor (*Velella velella*) — 67, 27

Sea anemones — 69, 28

93. Red beadlet (*Actinia tenebrosa*) — 69, 28
94. Striped anemone (*Epiactis thomsoni*) — 69, 28
95. Wandering anemone (*Phlytenactis tuberculosa*) — 69, 28

Sponges — 71, 29

96. Finger sponge (*Callyspongia ramosa*) — 71, 29
97. Slaty sponge (*Ancorina alata*) — 71, 29

Seaweeds (*Algae*) — 73, 30

99. Sawtoothed comb weed (*Marginariella boryana*) — 73, 30
100. Flapjack (*Carpophyllum maschalocarpum*) — 73, 30
101. Flexible flapjack (*Carpophyllum flexuosum*) — 73, 30
102. Bull kelp (*Durvillea antarctica*) — 75, 31
103. Bladder kelp (*Macrocystis pyrifera*) — 75, 31
104. Paddle weed (*Ecklonia radiata*) — 75, 31
105. Venus necklace (*Hormosira banksi*) — 77, 32
106. Comb weed (*Pterocladia lucida*) — 77, 32
107. Branching velvet weed (*Codium fragile*) — 77, 32
108. Sea rimu (*Caulerpa browni*) — 77, 32

INTRODUCTION

This book aims to give an introduction to some of the common and especially interesting plants and animals which are found around our shores. In a book of this kind, only examples of the major groups of marine plants and animals can be mentioned. Fishes will be covered in a companion volume, so are not treated here.

New Zealand supports an amazing variety of marine life for its size, and many of the species that live here are found nowhere else in the world. Some of them have developed structures and habitats which make them unique in their groups. However, even at this stage in our history, plants and animals which live in harbours and estuaries are threatened by reclamation of their marine habitats and by pollution. To understand something of their habits and environment is to provide a key for understanding the need for their protection.

In a country which, even without considering the southern islands, covers a wide range of latitudes from North Cape to Stewart Island, it is not surprising to find that all plants and animals do not occur throughout. Some have a wide distribution but many others live only in restricted areas. Not all the organisms illustrated here will therefore be found at every locality in New Zealand, but allied forms will generally be present.

Although many organisms live only in the intertidal zone and are exposed as the tide falls, others seldom or never enter this zone. To see these species we must rely on those which wash up along the coasts after storms or are brought up in fishing nets. The use of a face mask and snorkel will, of course, open up a new world — even if we venture only a few metres from the shore. The area around low-tide mark has in fact proven to be one of the richest in its variety of plant and animal life.

THE INTERTIDAL

The area between high- and low-water marks on any New Zealand coast is an exciting place. The plants and animals that live here must adapt to a wide range of conditions. Life here is not easy. Organisms are exposed to the air for varying periods twice each 24 hours and need to withstand the drying effects of wind and sun, extremes of temperature, flooding by fresh water, predators from the sea when the tide is in and predators from the land when the tide is out. The intertidal is also the area on which wave action is most strongly felt.

The result may be that the organism is perfectly adapted to a narrow range of conditions (even if at a dead end on the biological scale), or it may be able to tolerate a wider set of conditions in the scale available to intertidal animals and so retain a greater capacity for adaptation and greater possibilities for success.

Both these extremes, together with the great range of variants between, provide us with infinite scope for study and appreciation. As well, the whole area is accessible and requires neither effort nor special equipment to enjoy. It is a boundary zone between two major realms which, because of tidal action, is laid bare for our enjoyment, interest and even amusement.

Many animals living between tide marks have, for greater security, sacrificed the ability to move as adults. By attaching themselves to rock or other surfaces they may be able to build firm defences around themselves. This mode of life is possible only in water with a rich supply of minute life floating in it — a natural soup. Animals belonging to many different groups have adapted themselves to this existence. The same general kind of adaptation is required, though this may be achieved in different ways. Basically, some method must be devised for causing a current of sea water to pass through the animals, carrying in food and dissolved oxygen, and carrying away carbon dioxide and other waste products and reproductive bodies. Animals of such divergent groups as barnacles, sponges, sea squirts and lamp shells; bivalved shellfish such as the rock oysters and mussels, and a few univalves such as the slipper shells and the tube worms create water currents which pass across "fishing nets" of one sort or another, where food organisms of the correct size are extracted and passed to the animal's mouth. At the same time the respiratory fluids take up oxygen from the sea water and pass carbon dioxide out in solution. Bodily wastes are usually released into the outgoing current so that they can be dispersed well away from the animal.

Reproduction could be a problem with male and female animals unable to move. In most cases eggs and sperm will be produced separately. Sperm may be carried to the eggs inside the parent, or sperms and eggs may be released, with fertilisation taking place in the outside sea water. The fertilised egg may be brooded inside the female, or it may be released shortly after fertilisation. In some of the fixed animals small males may come to live closely associated with the female to ensure easy fertilisation. This happens in some bivalves and in univalves like the slipper limpets.

Fixed animals can protect themselves by heavy, limy, outside skeletons, as in the shellfish, lamp shells or barnacles; or with a flexible, tough coat as on the sea squirts. Some, like the sea anemones, may camouflage themselves with a covering of sand and shell fragments.

Some animals become fixed without achieving a water current of their own, either by utilising the work of the tides and the eddies in the sea, or by catching prey that swims into a "fishing net" — as do sea anemones, whose tentacles are complete with stinging cells. In some cases the animal may solve the problem of creating a water current by living in rock crevices through which the sea will run, thus providing an independent current. The stalked barnacle seems to be adapted to such conditions, the extended, finely jointed limbs being held out as a "fishing net".

DRYING OUT

Almost all the plants and animals which live between tide marks have been adapted to life in sea water. Such important life processes as respiration, food collection and reproduction are all dependent on being surrounded by water. In addition, organisms which are adapted to a life continuously surrounded by sea water need no special structures to prevent drying out. Those organisms which can successfully establish themselves in the intertidal zone must either already have some mechanism for preventing the body from drying out, or they must acquire one, as well as being able to keep enough water around themselves to maintain vital processes.

Some plants and animals in fact survive only in rock pools between the tide marks. This habitat does not require any major adaptation, for rock pools at low-tide mark are similar to the open sea. As rock pools occur at higher and higher levels towards high-tide mark, the number of plants and animals they can support decreases rapidly. High tidal pools can become very hot when exposed on a summer day, and very cold on a frosty night. In addition the salt content may be drastically reduced in heavy rain storms. Only those organisms which can withstand such changes will survive in this habitat.

Many animals burrow into rock, live in rock crevices or shelter under rocks or sheets of mussels, among rock oysters or in thick masses of seaweed. Besides offering protection from enemies, such habitats retain moisture, or actual sea water, for the periods during which they are exposed by the tides. However, there is too little oxygen available in the water they retain to allow violent activity, and most animals, whatever adaptation they may have to conserve water, will have to pass through the period between tides in a state of minimum activity. Many animals seal themselves within a tight-fitting, exterior skeleton which retains enough water inside. Thus oysters, mussels and other bivalves, barnacles and some tube worms use a limy protection. Many univalves such as the cat's eye seal themselves off with an operculum. Even the limpet-shaped shells can retain water within their shells by clamping themselves to the rock. Others, such as the sea squirts, have an exterior, flexible covering which serves the same purpose. Crabs have the gills set in protected pouches which are filled with sea water.

Many of these adaptations serve as a protection not only from enemies but also from the special destroyer of intertidal animals — heavy wave action. Burrowing or hiding in crevices, under stones or in seaweeds are good ways of avoiding being eaten or washed away. Conical flattened forms with wide attachment areas — as seen in limpets, barnacles, starfish or paua — are ideal for breaking wave action. Cementing the skeleton to the rocks, as do the barnacles and rock oysters; using attachment discs as do the limpets, or using sucker feet as do the sea anemones is also effective. Flexible, leathery bodies with tough attachments — as seen in the brown kelps and the sea tulip — help to cut down the dangers from crashing waves.

Forms of protection against enemies range from keeping out of the way to the use of heavy, limy castles (as in barnacles), or of armoured tanks (as in the chitons). The use of protective colouration or of active camouflage may be seen in many forms, from the spider crabs which grow seaweeds on their backs, to sea anemones which cover themselves with shell fragments. Other animals are armed with spines (sea urchins), stings (sea anemones) or claws (crabs).

FEEDING

In the sea, as on land, only plants can build up organic substances from inorganic chemicals. Using the energy source of the sun, the marine plants produce all the food substances that can be utilised by animals. But the plants in the sea comprise a good deal more than the visible seaweeds of the coasts and shallow waters. Important as the seaweeds may be, they account for only a portion of the organic food substances needed to sustain the enormous animal populations of the sea. The most important plants there are the tiny diatoms. These small, single-celled plants, either floating or occurring in films on rocks, mud flats, the underside of ice floes, or even in such unlikely places as on the skin of whales, supply the basic bricks upon which the major part of the food chains in the sea are built. The statement that "all flesh is grass" has been matched with "all fish is diatom". It is the diatoms that supply the main soup course on which the animal plankton is nourished. The combination of plant and animal plankton, in one size range or another, is the basic food material for all the animals — even the intertidal ones which have sacrificed mobility for security and have become sedentary.

Thus in the sea, besides the straightout herbivores (the chewers and scrapers of seaweeds) and the carnivores (the chewers and swallowers of flesh), there is the other highly important group of plankton filterers. They are well represented in the intertidal. A fourth group found on land, but seldom mentioned in discussions on feeding in animals, is the detritus or compost-feeding group. These too are well represented in the sea, particularly where films of exceedingly rich organic material are deposited on mud flats.

HABITATS ON THE SHORE

Anyone who wishes to find any particular animal must know the exact habitat in which to look. Some animals have a very precise requirement and will be found only when these exact conditions occur. Some sea slugs, for example, feed only on one food and will be found nowhere else. Other animals are less tied to a narrow range of conditions, or the conditions that suit them are perhaps found over a wide range of habitats.

A basic division may be made between "hard" and "soft" shores — rocky shores and the realms of sand and mud. This is a deep-seated ecological distinction. Subdivision of these two major types of habitat may be made on the basis of the degree of exposure to wave action. Apart from muddy shores which are developed only in sheltered harbours or estuaries, rock or sand may run from extreme shelter to extreme exposure. On the whole, on "soft" shores, be they mud or sand, or a combination of both, in shelter or on open coast, the majority of the animals live in burrows, particularly when the tide is out. On mud and sand flats, enormous numbers of the same species of animal may be developed to a much more marked degree than on rocky coastlines, where a much greater variety of species may be expected.

HOW TO FIND ANIMALS

Many animals which live in the intertidal area are not obvious at first glance. Many hide themselves away from light, hot sun or from their enemies. Others camouflage themselves or mask their appearance. Those that are obvious — the barnacles, the limpets, the cat's eye shells and the chitons — are anchored securely to the rock surface with a heavy outside skeleton for protection. Most other animals will find shelter when the tide is out by creeping beneath stones or seaweeds, by disappearing into rocks and crevices, or even by burrowing into the sand or rock pools.

To find many of them we must be prepared to turn stones and rocks over at all levels between tide marks, and to probe into crevices and crannies. At the same time we must always remember that interfering with habitats is likely to cause great disturbance to many plants and animals. We should remedy any disturbance we create as carefully as possible. Having turned a rock over and observed the creatures living or sheltering beneath it, we should replace it in its original position and take care not to crush everything under it.

Animals that live on sandy beaches or on mud flats seldom stay on the surface when the tide is out but burrow to various depths. On sandy beaches the presence of animals living beneath the surface will often be revealed by the marks made by siphons or the entrances to burrows. A good method of finding some of these animals is to strain some of the mud or sand through a sieve. Sometimes a surprising number of animals will be produced.

Although many animals live in tide pools, they are not always obvious either on the stones or sand which often line the pools or in the seaweeds around the edge.

A good selection of the plants and animals which live below low-tide mark can often be examined when washed ashore, especially after storms. Many strange creatures from a variety of habitats may come together in the drift towards low-tide mark.

Many seaweeds and animals do not show their full beauty of form when the tide is out. Sometimes we can see their more delicate structures or get them to uncoil if we place them in the clear water of a rock pool. Better still, place a sea anemone, a small sea urchin, a sea slug, a common shrimp, a young paua, or one of the delicate red seaweeds in a preserving jar of fresh sea water and watch from the side.

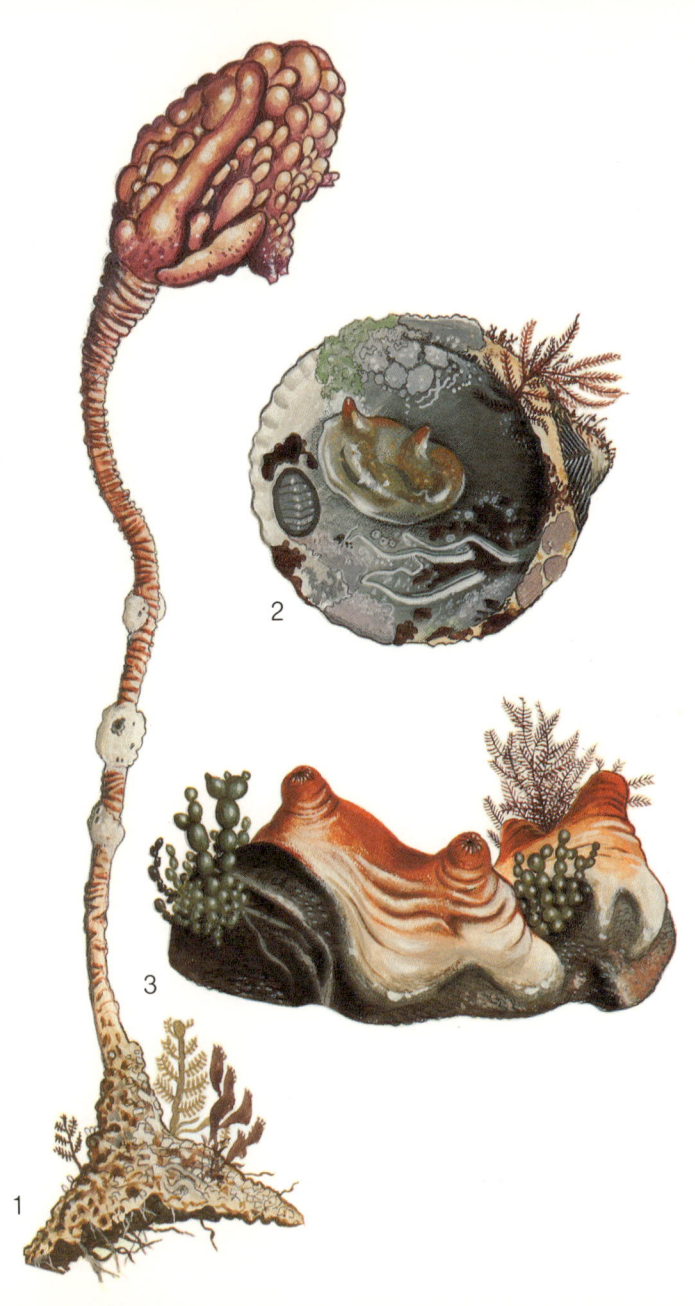

SEA SQUIRTS (Tunicates or Ascidians)

Sea squirts are rather shapeless, leathery animals with two siphons. Adults live attached to rocks, dead shells or to seaweeds. Water is drawn through one siphon, passes through a delicate sieve inside the animal and moves out through the other siphon. This current of water brings food and oxygen to the animal. If it is gently squeezed, a sea squirt will often squirt a stream of water through a siphon like a jet from a water pistol.

1. **Sea tulip** (*Pyura pachydermatina*)
Common from Cook Strait southwards, this stalked sea squirt lives on rocky shores amongst larger seaweeds, often in enormous numbers. The long, flexible stalk allows it to bend to the force of the waves.

2. **Transparent sea squirt** (*Corella eumyota*)
One of the commonest sea squirts throughout New Zealand, it lives fixed under stones or empty shells between tide marks. The body is almost completely transparent but the two siphons are coloured a reddish-orange.

3. **Saddle sea squirt** (*Cnemidiocarpa bicornuta*)
Many of the sea squirts found around low-tide mark have this saddle shape with the siphons forming two horns. The outside skin is tough and flexible. Some kinds may be covered by mud or silt, or by other marine growths, and may then be very difficult to detect.

Plate 1

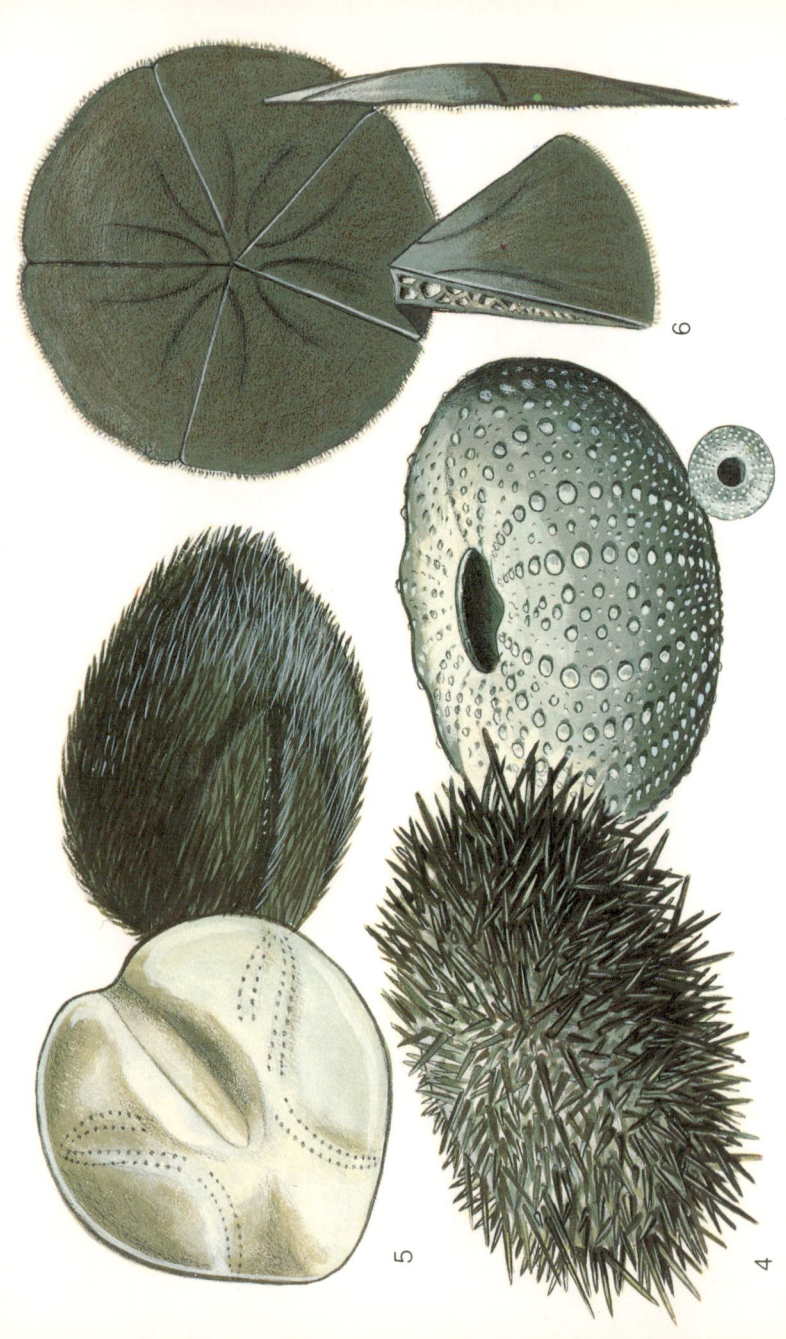

SEA URCHINS

Sea urchins belong to one of the groups of spiny-skinned animals called echinoderms. The three illustrated here all have a limy skeleton underneath a layer of spines, and each lives in a very different habitat.

4. **Common sea urchin, sea egg or kina** (*Evechinus chloroticus*)
In life the skeleton bears many rather long, sharp spines which can swivel easily on a ball-and-socket joint. If a living sea urchin is placed in a jar of sea water, narrow, dark tubes will push out through the spines. These are the tube feet which are forced out in rows by water pressure inside the animal and help the animal to move along. The common sea urchin lives under ledges at low-tide mark, but its skeleton often washes ashore.

5. **Heart urchin** (*Echinocardium cordatum*)
Heart urchins live in burrows on the muddy floors of sheltered harbours, often in enormous numbers. The dried skeleton is very fragile and only occasionally washes ashore whole, even though thousands may be living only a few hundred metres away. The spines are short and rather brittle.

6. **Cake urchin, sand dollar or snapper biscuit** (*Fellaster zelandicus*)
Cake urchins live at low tide and below on open, sandy beaches. The dried skeleton easily breaks into five segments, the broken edges showing a very complicated limy structure inside. The spines are tiny and are easily brushed off.

Plate 2

STARFISHES

Like sea urchins, the starfishes are built on a five-rayed plan, although some starfishes have many more than five arms. The skin is set with limy plates, and the mouth is situated on the underside in the centre of the arms.

7. **Biscuit star** (*Pentagonaster pulchellus*)
One of our most beautiful starfishes, the colour pattern varies from tinted red through orange to grey or even light purple. The body is very stiff and the whole rim is lined with large, solid plates. It occurs from about East Cape southwards.

8. **Cushion star** (*Patiriella regularis*)
This is the most common intertidal starfish throughout New Zealand. Again the colour varies, but mottled green shades are the most usual. Although the usual number of arms is five, occasional examples are found with four or even as many as eight arms.

9. **Reef star** (*Stichaster australis*)
A large starfish, which reaches a span of about 35 cm, the reef star lives on open, exposed, rocky coasts. The animal is strong and clings solidly to the rocks. The number of arms varies but there are usually ten, eleven or twelve.

BRITTLESTARS

10. **Mottled sand star** (*Ophionereis fasciatus*)
This sand star and the following species belong to a group of echinoderms called brittlestars. They differ from the starfishes in that they have a small, round, central disc from which the arms radiate. The arms often break very easily if the animals are disturbed, but they will grow again. The mottled sand star is extremely common under stones on sand near low-water mark.

11. **Oar sand star** (*Ophiopteris antipodum*)
In this sand star, spines are arranged like banks of oars in rows alongside the arms. It is found throughout most of New Zealand under stones resting on sand towards low-water mark.

SEA CUCUMBER

12. **Common sea cucumber** (*Stichopus mollis*)
This represents a further large group of echinoderms in which the body has become sausage-shaped, with the limy plates of the skeleton set in the skin. It is our largest common sea cucumber and lives in pools amongst stones and weeds. If disturbed, it throws out sticky white threads, and if handled will often push out its whole stomach.

CHITONS OR COAT AND MAIL SHELLS

Chitons are one of the five main groups into which the shellfish are divided. In this group, the shell consists of eight overlapping plates bound together by a flexible, leathery girdle. The whole animal is thus very flexible in movement, but can cling firmly to rocks without ever exposing the animal's flesh. Specimens with more or fewer than eight plates (or valves) are extremely rare.

13. **Noble chiton** (*Eudoxochiton nobilis*)
Our largest chiton, the noble chiton reaches a length of about 10 cm and lives at or below low-water mark on rocky coasts.

14. **Snake's skin chiton** (*Sypharochiton pelliserpentis*)
The commonest New Zealand chiton, the snake's skin chiton lives in large numbers between tide marks — even on exposed, bare rocks. The shell surface is often eroded.

15. **Butterfly Chiton** (*Cryptoconchus porosus*)
Found throughout New Zealand from about low water down to moderate depth, the butterfly chiton does not at first appear to have any shell at all. Down the middle of the back is a row of narrow slits through which the eight valves can just be seen. The girdle almost completely covers the valves. Each valve when separated has the shape of a butterfly, the colour being mainly whitish. The girdle colour varies considerably.

16. **Variable Chiton** (*Ischnochiton maorianus*)
Very common under stones from about half tide downwards, this chiton occurs in a wide range of colour patterns. It moves quite rapidly when exposed to light and immediately seeks shelter.

Plate 5

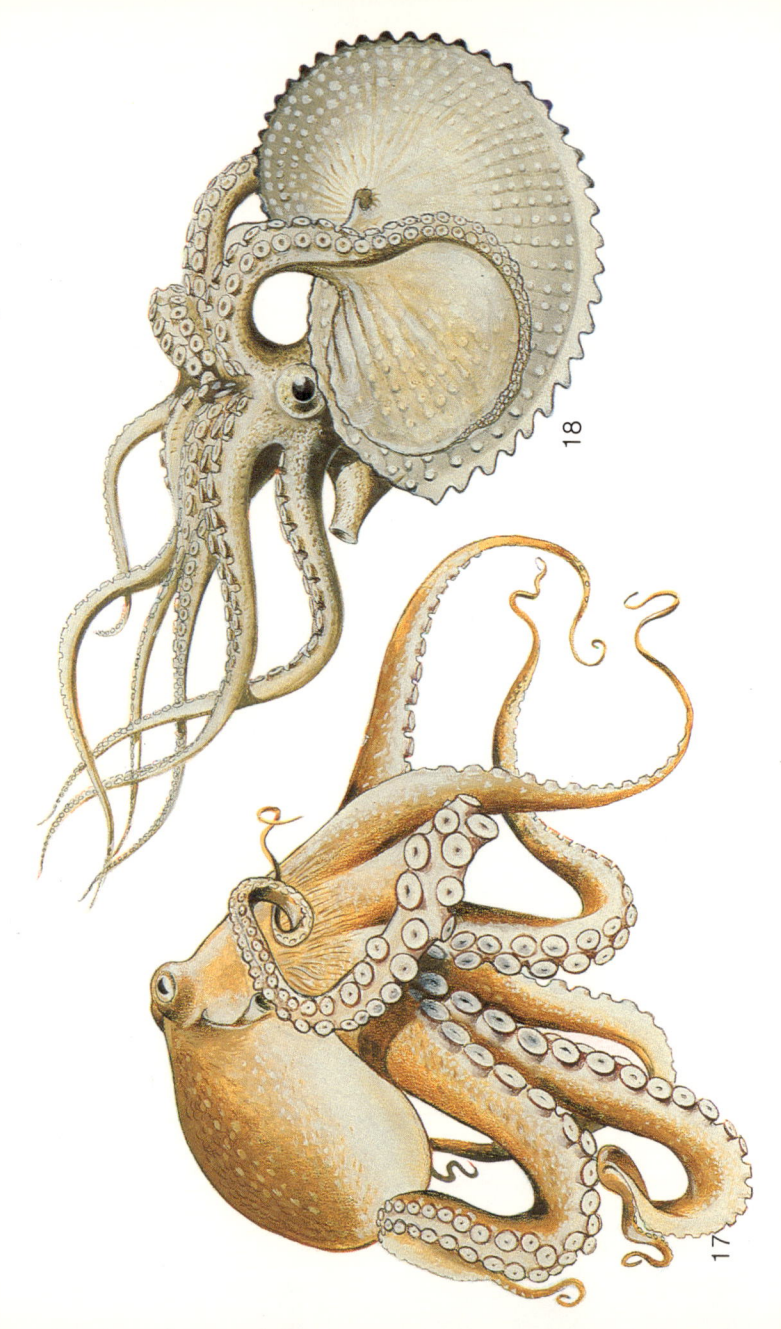

SQUIDS, OCTOPUSES AND THEIR ALLIES
(Cephalopoda)

Although the shell is usually absent or, at most, an internal remnant, these creatures represent another of the five groups of shellfish. They are divided into two main groups: the octopuses and their allies, with eight arms and no real shells, and the squids (together with the cuttle fish), which have an additional pair of long tentacles and usually an internal shell of some kind. These animals have muscular bodies and can move quickly. The eyes are very well developed, there is a strong siphon which gives them jet propulsion, and most can squirt out a cloud of ink to mislead their attackers.

17. **Common octopus** (*Octopus maorum*)
Common throughout New Zealand, our only large octopus seldom has arms longer than 1 m, and even at this length the arms are quite slender. It appears to be a rather timid animal. Females stay close to their eggs and squirt sea water over them until they hatch.

18. **Paper nautilus** (*Argonauta nodosa*)
The remarkably beautiful "shell" is formed only by the female as a brood chamber for the eggs and developing young. The male is quite small and is seldom seen. Paper nautilus live on the surface of the open sea well away from land, but the shells sometimes come ashore during the summer.

SQUIDS, OCTOPUSES AND THEIR ALLIES
continued

19. **Broad-finned squid** (*Sepioteuthis bilineata*)
This is one of our two common squid species, recognised by the oval-shaped fin which runs right round the body. It is more commonly found in harbours.

20. **Arrow squid** (*Notodarus sloani*)
The fin is rather short and shaped rather like the head of an arrow. This squid occurs in schools in the open sea and is the species on which our squid fishing industry is based.

21. **Jewelled squid** (*Sepioloidea pacifica*)
Although common throughout New Zealand this little squid is seldom seen. It lives in a variety of habitats but usually shelters on the bottom during the day. It is sometimes caught in drag nets in harbours.

22. **Ram's horn squid** (*Spirula spirula*)
The open spiral shell, divided into airtight compartments, washes ashore in its thousands on our beaches, although the animal that forms it lives in the intermediate depths over very deep sea far from land. In the living animal, the shell, which is internal, gives buoyancy like the air tanks of a submarine.

Plate 7

BIVALVES

In the bivalve shellfish the shell is formed by two valves hinged together along the top. Most feed by filtering plankton from the sea water.

23. **Green edged mussel** (*Perna canaliculus*)
Our largest true mussel grows to about 18 cm in length. Young shells are bright emerald-green in colour but darken as the shells grow. Most mussels attach themselves to rocks and other objects by a series of fine threads called a byssus (or beard). This is the main species used as a food in New Zealand.

24. **Black edged mussel** (*Mytilus edulis aoteanus*)
Smaller than the green edged mussel, this species is most common in the south. The inside of the shell is marked with broad, navy blue blotches.

25. **Horse mussel** (*Atrina zelandica*)
This is our largest bivalve shellfish, growing up to 33 cm in length, though usually not more than 18 cm. The shell is thin and brittle and shines with iridescent colours. Horse mussels live at or below low-tide mark, usually in harbours or in sheltered waters. Broken shells are often washed ashore. In life, the pointed end is buried deep in sandy mud with only 3 cm or so of the fragile, curved end exposed. In addition to a small bunch of fine byssus threads, the rows of short, hollow tubes along the upper edge of the shell help to keep it anchored.

Plate 8

BIVALVES continued

26. **Nesting mussel** (*Modiolarca impacta*)
In this mussel the threads of the byssus form a nest (rather like a cocoon), inside which a whole colony of nesting mussels may live attached to rocks and gravel, at and below low-tide mark.

27. **Ribbed mussel** (*Aulacomya maorianus*)
This species, which is more common in the south, seldom grows to an edible size. It is often found living in cracks and crevices on open, rocky coasts.

28. **Common scallop** (*Pecten novaezelandiae*)
The shape of the common scallop, with its one flat valve and one concave valve, is well known. The animal is one of our prized sea foods. The animal has two rows of eyes around the edge of the mantle and these can detect the approach of enemies. By opening and shutting the shells rapidly, the scallop can swim in a jerky fashion and so often escapes from danger. Scallops are found throughout New Zealand, but are concentrated enough to support a commercial harvest only in a few places.

29. **Fan scallop** (*Chlamys zelandiae*)
Several kinds of fan scallop live in New Zealand waters. The shells display a wide range of colours and the variations are prized by shell collectors. Fan scallops live attached by fine byssus threads to the undersides of stones and are common throughout the North Island. A very similar scallop in the South Island lives covered in sponge.

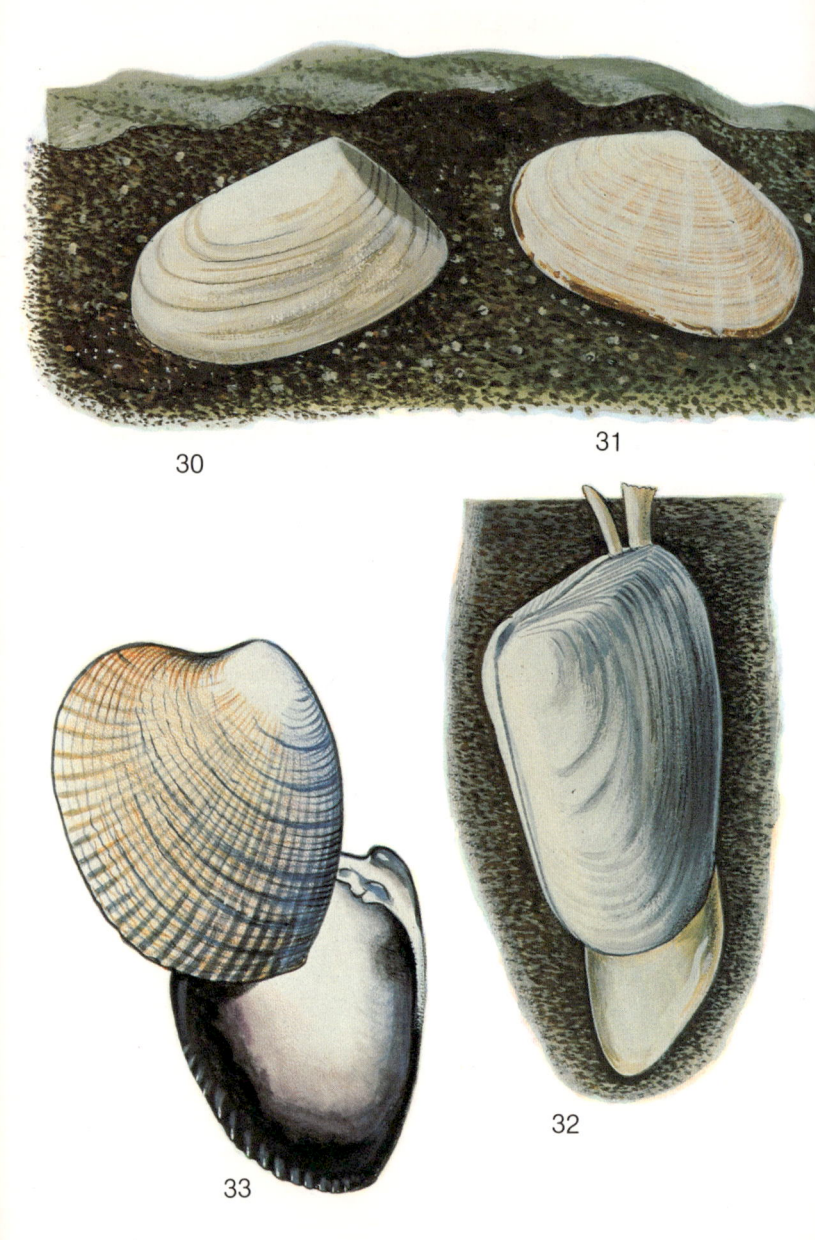

BIVALVES continued

30. **Tuatua** (*Paphies (Mesodesma) subtriangulatum*)
Three species of this group of bivalves occur commonly in New Zealand and all are edible. Tuatuas live on open, sandy beaches towards low-tide mark, often tightly packed together. The shell grows up to about 8 cm in length. Two forms occur, the one most common in the north has a shell like the one illustrated, while the southern form has the beak nearer the middle of the shell. Both forms occur on the west coast beaches near Wellington.

Before cooking, it is advisable to leave the shellfish in a bucket of sea water overnight to remove the sand.

31. **Pipi** (*Paphies australis*)
The pipi occurs plentifully throughout New Zealand, living in sandy mud in harbours and estuaries, often close to beds of the common cockle. It is smaller than the tuatua and is oval in shape. Although providing good food, it is becoming increasingly difficult to find beds of large shells in unpolluted habitats.

32. **Toheroa** (*Paphies (Mesodesma) ventricosa*)
One of the best known of the edible shellfish, the toheroa is rapidly decreasing in numbers and has to be protected by the enforcement of a short annual "season", when a restricted number can be taken. They live deeply buried at about half-tide mark on open, sandy beaches, and can burrow actively in the sand. Although found throughout most of New Zealand, they have been common only along the west coast of the North Island and on some beaches in Foveaux Strait. Old dead shells measuring 30 cm have been found in the north, but living examples grow not much more than 18 cm long.

33. **New Zealand or common cockle** (*Austrovenus stutchburyi*)
Another most edible shellfish, the cockle lives in harbour mud flats and in estuaries throughout New Zealand. Like the pipi, the cockle suffers from pollution of the habitat. The purple colour inside the shell is characteristic.

Plate 10

BIVALVES continued

34. **Coarse dosinia** (*Dosinia anus*)
Five species of *Dosinia* occur in New Zealand but only three are commonly seen. All are perfectly circular in outline and differ mainly in the strength of the circular ridges which decorate the outside of the shell. The coarse dosinia is the largest species (about 70 mm across) and lives buried in the sand on open, sandy beaches from low-tide mark downwards.

35. **Frilled Venus shell** (*Bassina yatei*)
One of our most beautiful bivalves, it has wide, frilled, concentric flanges which anchor the shell in muddy sand. It lives below low-tide mark and is therefore only seen when the shell is washed ashore.

36. **Morning star** (*Tawera spissa*)
This small (about 30 mm) bivalve is sometimes incredibly common off our sandy beaches and is often washed ashore. The shells are marked by intricate, brown colour patterns, often arranged in a zig-zag. No two patterns are exactly alike.

37. **Rock borer** (*Anchomas similis*)
Three very similar rock borers live embedded in holes which they dig in soft sandstone rock — leaving only small exterior holes through which the siphons can suck water. The shells of all three are fragile and white. When the two dead valves are opened out they look like a pair of wings, and some of these rock borers are called angel's wings.

BIVALVES continued

38. **Large wedge shell** (*Macomona liliana*)
Wedge shells can be recognised by one edge of the shell being twisted to the side. Large wedge shells live deeply buried in harbour mud flats with the long siphons reaching up to the surface. Live shells are therefore seldom seen, but dead shells are often washed ashore. Wedge shells feed by sucking up the thin layer of rich, compost-like detritus from the surface of the mud flats with the siphons.

39. **Triangle shell** (*Spisula aequilateralis*)
With the most regular triangular shape of all the bivalves and growing to about 50 mm in length, this species lives on exposed sandy beaches just below low tide. After storms the shells may be washed ashore in their thousands.

40. **Rock oyster** (*Crassostrea glomerata*)
Entirely northern in distribution, the rock oyster does not naturally extend further south than Tauranga. Rock oysters attach themselves by cementing one valve to rocks, often forming a thick ribbon of oysters. The shell is marked by the crenulations around the edge of the valves and by purple shadings on the inside of the shell. This is the species used in oyster farming in New Zealand.

41. **Dredge oyster or Stewart Island oyster** (*Ostrea lutaria*)
Although found throughout New Zealand from low-tide mark downwards, the dredge oyster is commercially plentiful only in a few areas like Golden Bay and Foveaux Strait.

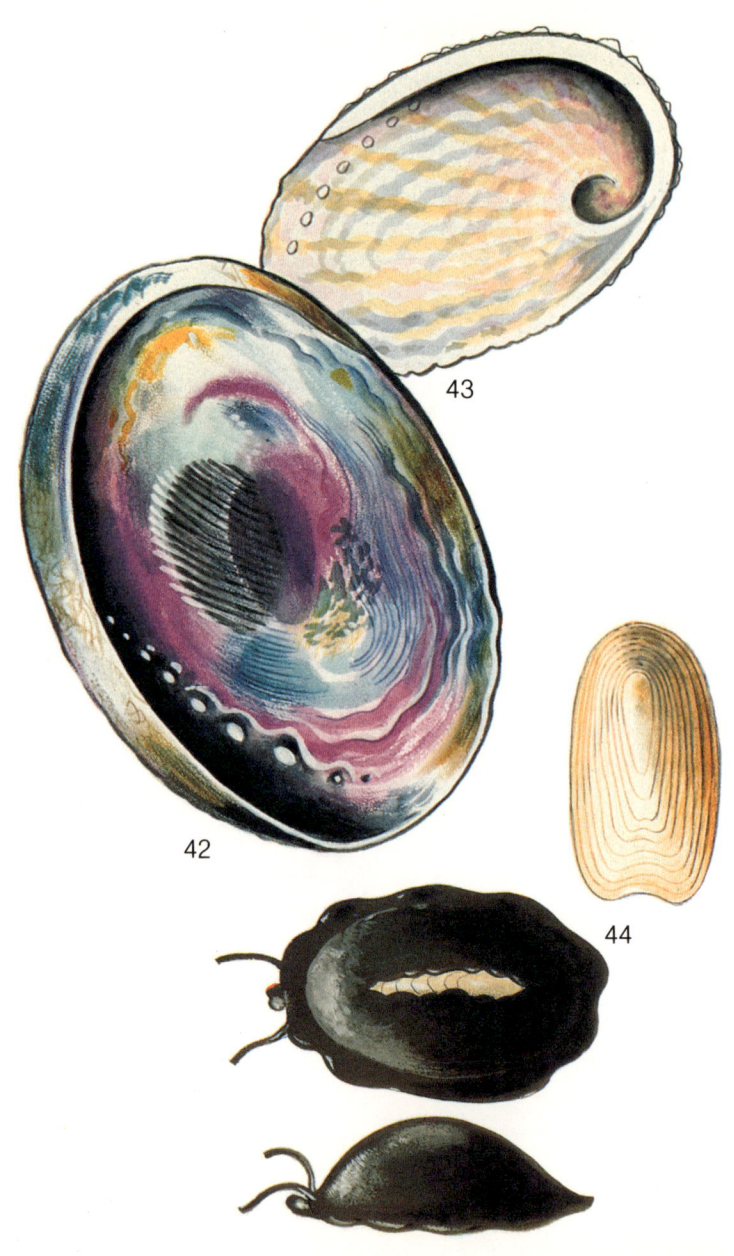

UNIVALVES

The largest group of shellfish is the one known as univalves or gastropods (stomach foot). Here the shell usually consists of a single piece or valve. This shell may be tent-shaped, as in the limpets; coiled into a tight spiral, like the whelk, or coiled in a flat spiral, like the paua. In some forms the shell is reduced, as in the shield shell; or it may have disappeared completely, as in the sea slugs. In many of the coiled forms, the mouth of the shell can be sealed off with a horny or a shelly "lid" known as the operculum.

42. **Paua** (*Haliotis iris*)

This well-known shellfish lives throughout New Zealand but is more common in the south. Young shells often live under stones near low-water mark but as they grow the shells migrate towards deeper water. Three species live in New Zealand, and similar species occur in Australia, Japan, California and in Europe.

43. **Pink paua** (*Haliotis australis*)

The pink paua may be recognised by its smaller size, all-over pinkish colour and the dimpled shell surface. The area between the row of holes and the edge of the shell bears three or more strong spiral ridges, but it is smooth in the larger paua.

44. **Shield shell** (*Scutus breviculus*)

The large, velvety, black animal almost completely covers the small, solid shell, which is shaped like an old Roman shield. The animal is very like that of the paua, and is sometimes mistaken for a paua which has lost its shell.

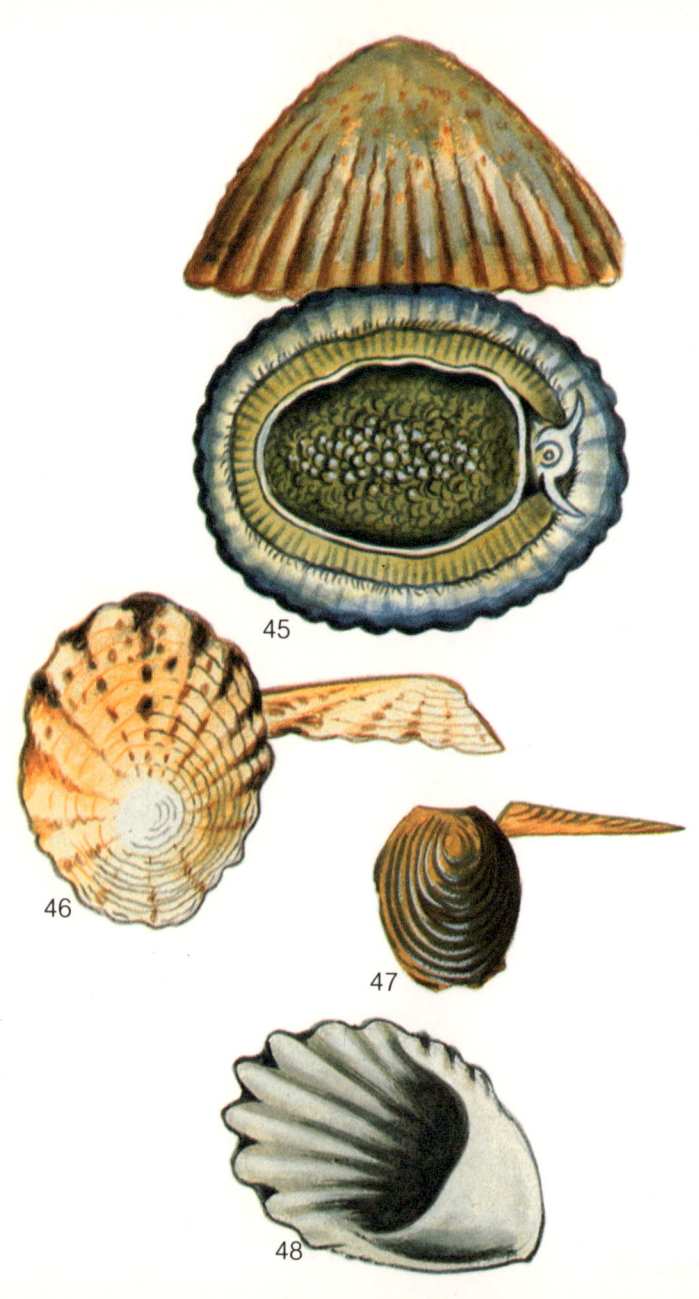

UNIVALVES continued

45. **Ornate limpet** (*Cellana ornata*)
At least two or three species of limpet occur on most rocky coasts. They live well up towards mid-tide line and are usually very obvious. All browse on small seaweeds and only become active when covered by the rising tide. The two commonest species are the ornate and the radiate limpets. Both are variable in shape but the ornate limpet is usually higher and more tent-shaped. The interior of the shell has a wide border of alternate dark and light colour bands around the edge.

46. **Radiate limpet** (*Cellana radians*)
This limpet is very variable in shape, in the size and number of the radial ribs and in colour and colour pattern. Some shells are very flat indeed. The shell surface is often corroded or covered with small barnacles. The interior of all the large limpets has a dark central patch corresponding to the shape of the animal, and a horse-shoe shaped ring which marks the line where the shell muscles were attached in life.

47. **Fragile limpet** (*Atalacmea fragilis*)
The fragile limpet is a representative of a large number of smaller limpets, some species of which occur in all parts of New Zealand. This clearly marked, very thin-shelled form lives underneath smooth stones towards high-tide mark, often in groups of ten or more. It grows to about 1.5 cm.

48. **Ribbed slipper limpet** (*Maoricrypta costata*)
Rather like a normal limpet from the outside, the shell has a flat plate across part of the interior — rather like the foot of a slipper. The outside has heavy ribs. It is usually found attached to other shells such as mussels. A related species has a completely smooth shell.

UNIVALVES continued

49. **Cunningham's tiger shell** (*Maurea selecta*)
Tiger shells are very characteristic New Zealand univalves. They range up to about 10 cm across and display interesting shell ornament and colour patterns. They are mainly found on rocky coastlines, but Cunningham's tiger shell lives on open, sandy, west coast beaches and is usually seen washed ashore after storms.

50. **Large tiger shell** (*Maurea tigris*)
The large tiger shell is found throughout New Zealand, usually on rocky coasts below low-tide mark, and in association with large brown seaweeds. The barred reddish-brown stripes give rise to its name. It is one of the shells most prized by collectors.

51. **Opal top shell** (*Cantharidus opalus*)
Most of our top shells are quite small (1 cm or less). The opal top shell, however, grows to about 5 cm and with its intricate colour pattern and highly iridescent mouth to the shell, it is particularly colourful. Like most of the top shells it lives attached to brown seaweeds throughout New Zealand.

52. **Black nerita** (*Nerita melanotragus*)
The black nerita is a common North Island shell which lives high up on intertidal rocks. With its habit of clumping together in groups and its dark navy blue shell, it is very obvious on open rock faces. It is often called a periwinkle by small children who boil them and pull them free from their shells with a pin for food.

Plate 15

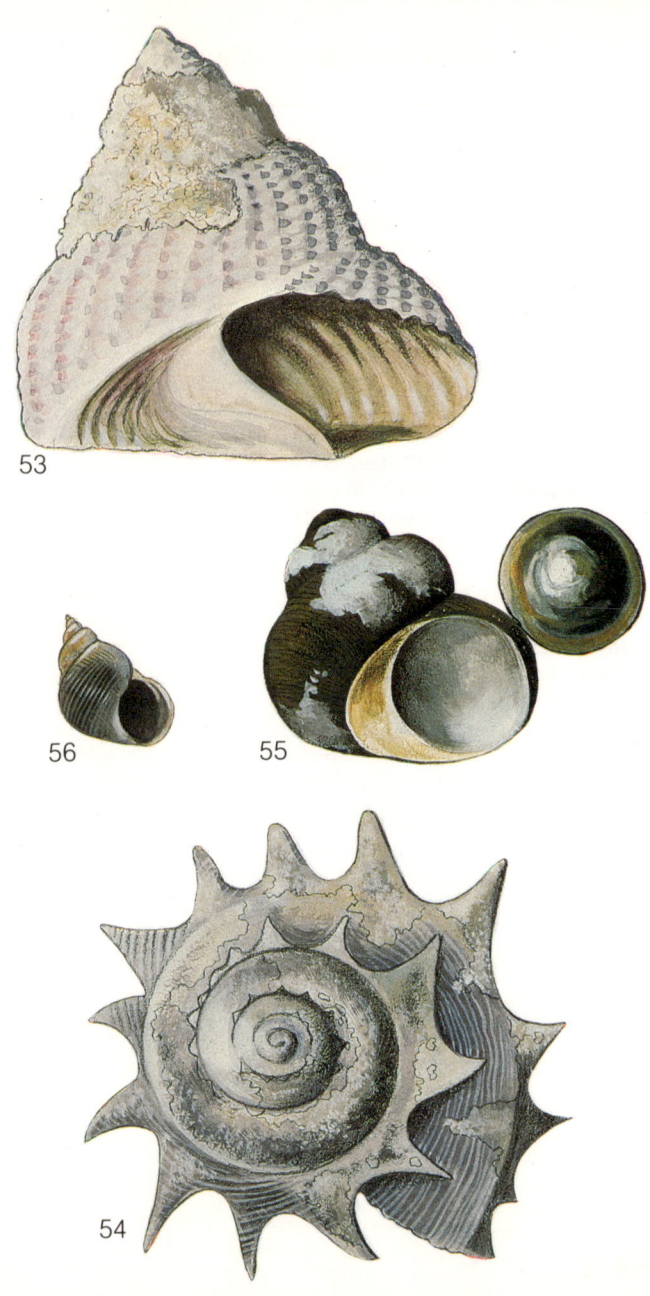

UNIVALVES continued

53. **Cook's turban shell** (*Cookia sulcata*)
Named after Captain Cook, whose explorations made many New Zealand shells known in Europe for the first time, this large (10 cm) shell lives along the coastlines of our main islands. Normally living on rocks below low-tide mark, the shell is often overgrown and dirty. When the shells die and are washed ashore, the pearly inside layer is often exposed. The operculum is large, heavy and shelly.

54. **Circular saw shell** (*Astraea heliotropium*)
Especially common in places south of Cook Strait, this shell is prized by collectors. Also known as the "spur shell" from its shape, some English writers claim it should be called "Captain Cook's imperial sun trochus", which would be rather a mouthful for a common name.

55. **Cat's eye** (*Turbo smaragdus*)
Extremely well known, especially for its circular, limy operculum which looks like a cat's eye, this shell is common throughout New Zealand. It lives between tide marks and is often plentiful on the brown seaweed, Venus necklace. The shell is heavy with a dark green coating. It may grow to 8 cm across but is usually no more than half this size.

56. **Large periwinkle** (*Littorina cincta*)
Together with the smaller blue-banded periwinkle, the large periwinkle lives on rocky shores at, or even well above, normal high-water mark. It often occurs in large numbers. Both forms occur throughout New Zealand.

Plate 16

UNIVALVES continued

57. **Large trumpet** (*Charonia lampas capax*)
Our largest univalve, the large trumpet is found throughout New Zealand at or below low-tide mark on rocky shores, although it is more common in the north. Specimens may reach a length of 26 cm but are usually smaller. Shells of this kind throughout the world have been used as shell trumpets, and the Maori made the same use of our species.

58. **Helmet shell** (*Xenophalium pyrum*)
The helmet shell lives on open sandy coasts throughout New Zealand and is often washed ashore. It normally grows to about 7 cm in length. Several allied species live in deeper water.

59. **Southern volute** (*Alcithoe swainsoni*)
Several species of volute shells live in New Zealand, and this is a group which is much sought after by collectors. Two species are common. The southern volute lives on open sandy beaches and has a streamlined shell with a row of small nodules for ornament. In more sheltered northern waters the Arabic volute (*Alcithoe arabica*) occurs with much stronger nodules and a darker colour pattern.

60. **Southern olive** (*Baryspira australis*)
Olive shells are relatively small, with completely streamlined, darkish shells which are covered by the animal in life. They live on sand and sandy muds. The most common species is the southern olive, which grows up to 4 cm in length and is found throughout the country.

Plate 17

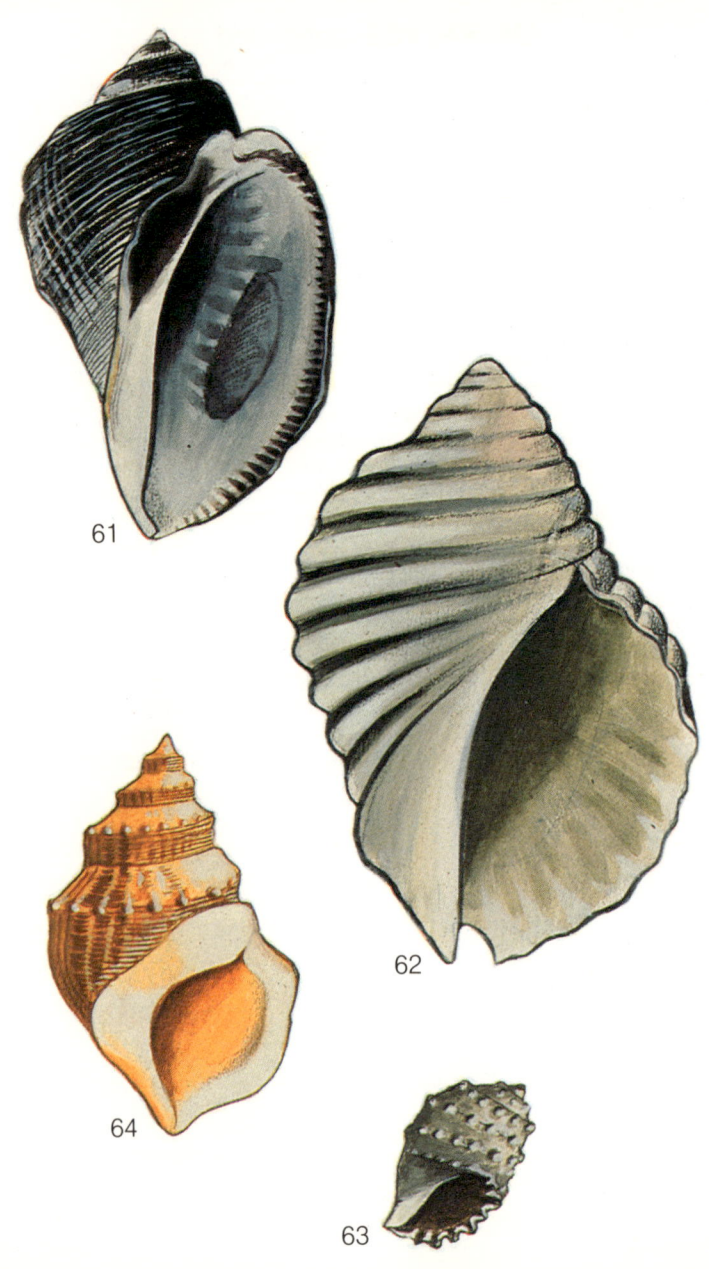

UNIVALVES continued

61. **Dark rock shell** (*Haustrum haustorium*)
Together with the oyster borer and its allies, the two rock shells illustrated here belong to one of the most rapacious carnivorous families of univalves. The dark rock shell lives on rocky coasts between tide marks. Its distribution is New Zealand wide, and it can be recognised by the expanded mouth to the shell, which is usually dark coloured inside.

62. **White rock shell** (*Thais orbita*)
This is a large, heavy shell which is usually dirty white in colour with a yellowish tinge inside the mouth. Some forms have heavy spiral ridges like the specimen illustrated, but others have much finer spirals. White rock shells live on rocky coasts in a variety of habitats, sometimes with many together in a group.

63. **Oyster borer** (*Lepsiella scobina*)
The oyster borer is extremely common between tide marks on rocky coasts throughout New Zealand. It feeds on small rock oysters in the north but particularly on the common, small intertidal barnacles. Using the tooth ribbon (radula), it bores a small hole through the shell of the prey and sucks out the animal.

64. **Large ostrich foot** (*Struthiolaria papulosa*)
A very characteristic New Zealand univalve, the large ostrich foot lives on sandy shores throughout New Zealand, usually below low tide. It was given its common name because the pointed edges of the mouth of the shell reminded early naturalists of the footprint of a large bird.

Plate 18

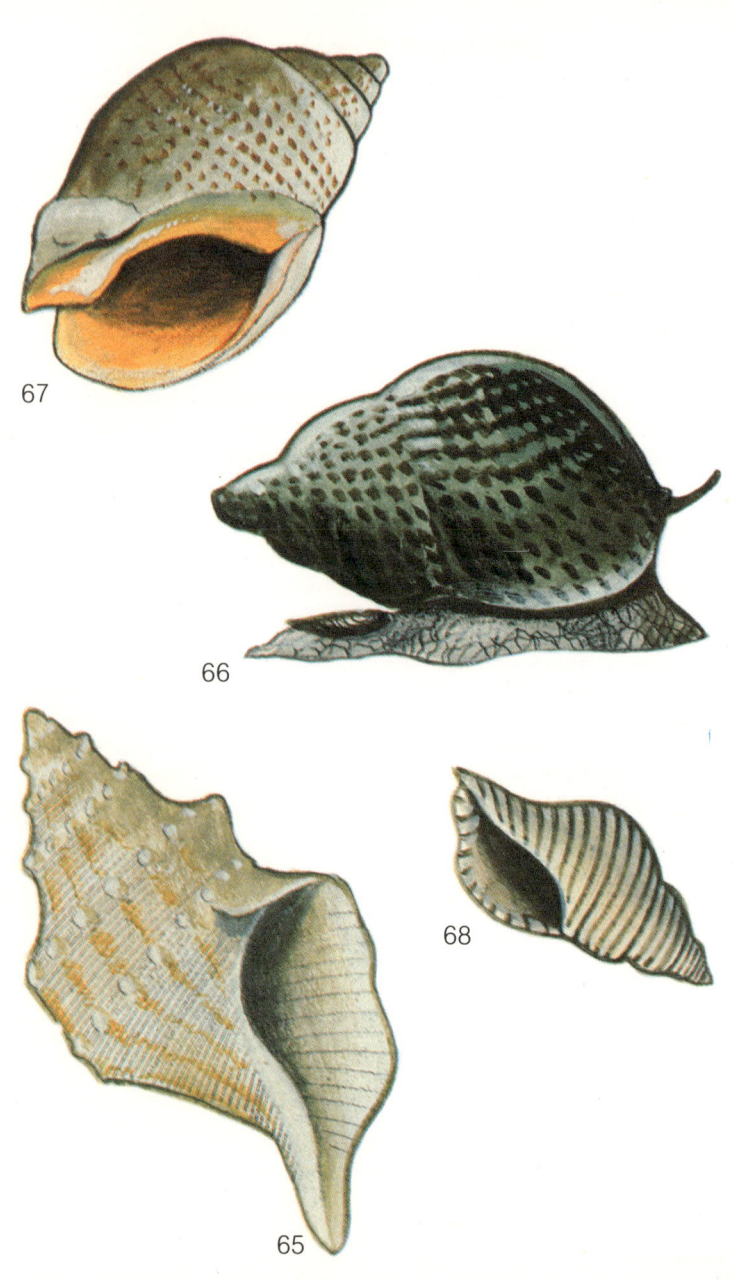

UNIVALVES continued

65. **Knobbed whelk** (*Austrofusus glans*)
Extremely common on sandy beaches, the knobbed whelk is often washed ashore with the large ostrich foot and is sometimes confused with young specimens of this species which have not yet developed the greatly thickened edge to the mouth of the shell. Some examples are very beautifully marked with patterns of brown lines and blotches.

66. **Spotted whelk** (*Cominella maculosa*)
This species, together with the speckled whelk, is very common on harbour mud flats, especially around banks of green sea grass. Both species are active carnivores and handfuls of both species may be found feeding on the remains of dead fish or other shellfish.

67. **Speckled whelk** (*Cominella adspersa*)
Although found plentifully on harbour mud flats, the speckled whelk also occurs in a wide range of other habitats. At times it is equally common on rocky shores and extends down into deeper waters. It is variable in shape and often has an eroded shell surface. The shell is usually bright yellow inside the mouth, and some shells become extremely thick and heavy.

68. **Lined whelk** (*Buccinulum powelli*)
The lined whelk belongs to a group of rather variable, medium-sized (up to 4 cm), carnivorous species, which will be found living under stones on almost any rocky shore locality throughout New Zealand. Most have a colour pattern of dark spiral lines.

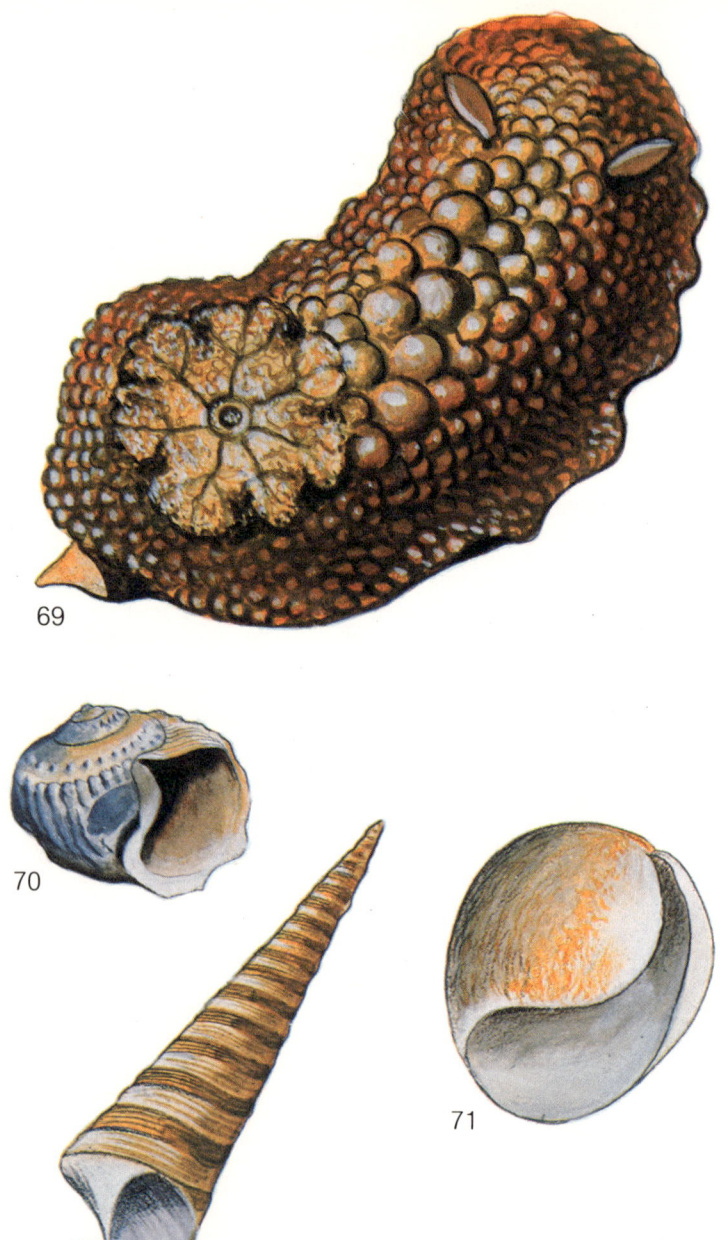

UNIVALVES continued

69. **Warty sea slug** (*Archidoris wellingtonensis*)
New Zealand has an amazing variety of sea slugs (univalves which have lost their shells), some of which have yet to be described. The warty sea slug is the largest, and grows up to about 12 cm in length. It is sometimes quite common on rocky coasts throughout New Zealand. The back is covered with large warts and the underside of the foot is bright orange. Some sea slugs are quite tiny and many are brilliantly coloured.

70. **Mud snail** (*Amphibola crenata*)
Mud flats in harbours and in estuaries may support thousands of these interesting though dull-looking snails. Mud snails feed by eating large amounts of surface mud, extracting the food material from it and leaving a continuous chain of detritus behind them.

71. **Fragile bubble shell** (*Haminoea zelandiae*)
This species has a very fragile shell which is largely covered by the animal in life. It is found throughout the North Island and the northern tip of the South Island amongst the green sea grass on mud flats.

72. **Turret shell** (*Maoricolpus roseus*)
Extremely common throughout New Zealand in the shallow water of harbours and off moderately sheltered coasts, the narrow, tightly coiled turret shell is usually seen when dead examples wash ashore.

CRUSTACEA

The great group of jointed-legged animals (Arthropods) includes, amongst others, the two large groups of insects (mostly on land) and crustacea (mostly in the sea). Crustacea have an external, jointed skeleton which covers the body and limbs like a suit of armour. They include a wide range of forms and sizes, from the crayfishes down to tiny forms no larger than a pinhead.

73. **Red rock crab** (*Plagusia chabrus*)
A large crab, which grows up to 8 cm or more across the back, the red rock crab lives in much the same habitat as the common crayfish and is often caught in crayfish pots. It becomes active at night and may venture out onto exposed rock platforms towards dusk. It can run swiftly and clings to the rock surface to prevent being washed away by the waves.

74. **Large shore crab** (*Leptograpsus variegatus*)
This crab, which grows up to about 5 cm across the back, is extremely common on rocky, exposed coasts. Here it ranges widely in search of food when the tide is out, moving rapidly on its long legs. When disturbed it retreats into protected cracks and crevices and presents its strong nippers to the intruder.

75. **Common rock crab** (*Hemigrapsus edwardsi*)
This is the crab most commonly found by people turning over rocks from towards high tide down to about half-tide mark on sheltered coasts throughout New Zealand. The back is about 4 cm across, and when disturbed the crab stands on its back legs and waves its nippers very aggressively. It is thus easily identified.

CRUSTACEA continued

76. **Hairy seaweed crab** (*Notomithrax ursus*)
This crab belongs to a family often called the camouflaged crabs because of their habit of covering their backs with seaweeds, sponges or other marine growths. The hairy seaweed crab is the most common species in the group and lives between tide marks. The back and legs are covered in stiff hairs into which the crab fits seaweed with its nippers. This seaweed often continues to grow and thus provides perfect camouflage. Like all other crabs, this species moults the whole outer skeleton several times during its life and after each moult it has to plant a new garden on its back.

77. **Common swimming crab** (*Ovalipes catharus*)
This large common crab reaches up to about 9 cm across the back. The last joint of the last pair of legs is flattened to form a paddle which can be used for swimming or as a shovel to dig the crab backwards into the sand. Here it will remain hidden with only the eyes and the antennae visible. Small examples are very common on sandy, west coast beaches.

78. **New Zealand cancer crab** (*Cancer novaezelandiae*)
Our cancer crab, which can grow up to 13 cm across the back, is closely allied to the European edible crab and similar species occur in many other parts of the world. Young examples live under stones towards low-water mark, but adults usually seek deeper water. The New Zealand form has much the same flavour as the European edible species but does not grow as large, nor does it seem to be plentiful enough to support commercial fishing.

Plate 22

CRUSTACEA continued

79. **Common crayfish** (*Jasus edwardsi*)
Only two species of marine crayfish are at all common in New Zealand: the common crayfish and the smoothtail. The common crayfish has rows of depressions across the tail segment to give a lobed appearance, the spines on the back are surrounded by rings of fine bristles while the general colour is a mottled deep purplish-red and orange. The smoothtail crayfish has relatively smooth tail segments, has no bristles around the spines on the back, the colour is much more uniform (usually dark green to yellowish-brown) and the skeleton is generally much smoother.

The common crayfish occurs throughout New Zealand.

80. **Smoothtail crayfish** (*Jasus verreauxi*)
This species also occurs in eastern Australia. Occasional specimens may grow very large (up to 18 kg) and these giants are known as packhorses. The smoothtail is not nearly as common as the common crayfish and is mainly found north of East Cape.

81. **Common shrimp** (*Palaemon affinis*)
This is the best known of our shrimps and prawns. Although it also lives below low-water mark, it is well adapted for life in rock pools. It makes a good aquarium animal and here its active, delicate feeding operation can be easily observed. If no better aquarium is available, it is worth keeping the shrimp in a preserving jar of sea water for an hour or so so that it can be watched from the side.

CRUSTACEA continued

82. **Half crab** (*Petrolisthes elongatus*)
Although the half crab looks very much like a normal crab, only four pairs of legs are visible from the top. The fifth pair is very small and can be seen only from the underside. If a specimen is held upside down it will often flap the curved-over tail as if it were swimming — a habit not seen in the true crabs. Half crabs are very common between tide marks throughout New Zealand and are frequently found in harbours and sheltered areas, where dozens may be found clustering under a single stone.

Another name for this group of crabs is "porcelain crab", a name which refers to the beautiful, porcelain-like colour and texture that crabs of this group often display on their backs. The New Zealand half crab shows this very well — the colour varying from a greenish-blue to greyish and even pinkish tones in some specimens.

The crab feeds by straining into its mouth small plants and animals from the sea water.

83. **Common hermit crab** (*Pagurus novaezelandiae*)
Hermit crabs use empty univalve shells as a protection for their own soft, twisted abdomens. One nipper is usually larger than the other and when the hermit crab pulls itself back into its borrowed shell, this nipper is bent to block off the mouth. Hermit crabs, like other crustacea, grow through several moults. With the casting off of the old skeleton, the hermit crab has to find another, slightly larger shell to use.

The common hermit crab is another good animal to keep in a small aquarium. Even when most of the animal seems still, the antennae, feelers and eyestalks will be constantly moving. It can be fed on small pieces of mussel or other shellfish.

Plate 24

BARNACLES

The external limy shell of the barnacle disguises the fact that the animal inside has the jointed legs of a crustacean. Only the larval stage can move about. Once the barnacle settles down and builds its first shell, it remains fixed for life.

84. **Goose barnacle** (*Lepas*)
Goose barnacles are often washed ashore. However, they normally live on the surface of the open sea, attached to almost anything that floats — logs of wood, bottles, fishing floats, pumice or drifting seaweed. Small specimens have even been found attached to the feet of penguins or the flippers of seals. The animal is protected by the jointed shell segments and is attached by a flexible stalk which can be bent and twisted. A large log covered by hundreds of these barnacles all writhing frantically can be a slightly alarming sight. The common name comes from the medieval myth that these barnacles grew into barnacle geese.

85. **Pink barnacle** (*Balanus decorus*)
This is the commonest of our large barnacles. It lives at low tide or below, often attached to shells — particularly dead ones inhabited by hermit crabs. Shells with the barnacles attached are often washed ashore after storms. The pink barnacle grows to about 4 cm across.

86. **Modest barnacle** (*Elminius modestus*)
One of the commonest small intertidal barnacles, the modest barnacle seldom grows more than 0.5 cm across. It is most frequently found in sheltered waters in harbours and estuaries and even grows on mangrove trunks in the north. It occurs less frequently on open coasts.

Plate 25

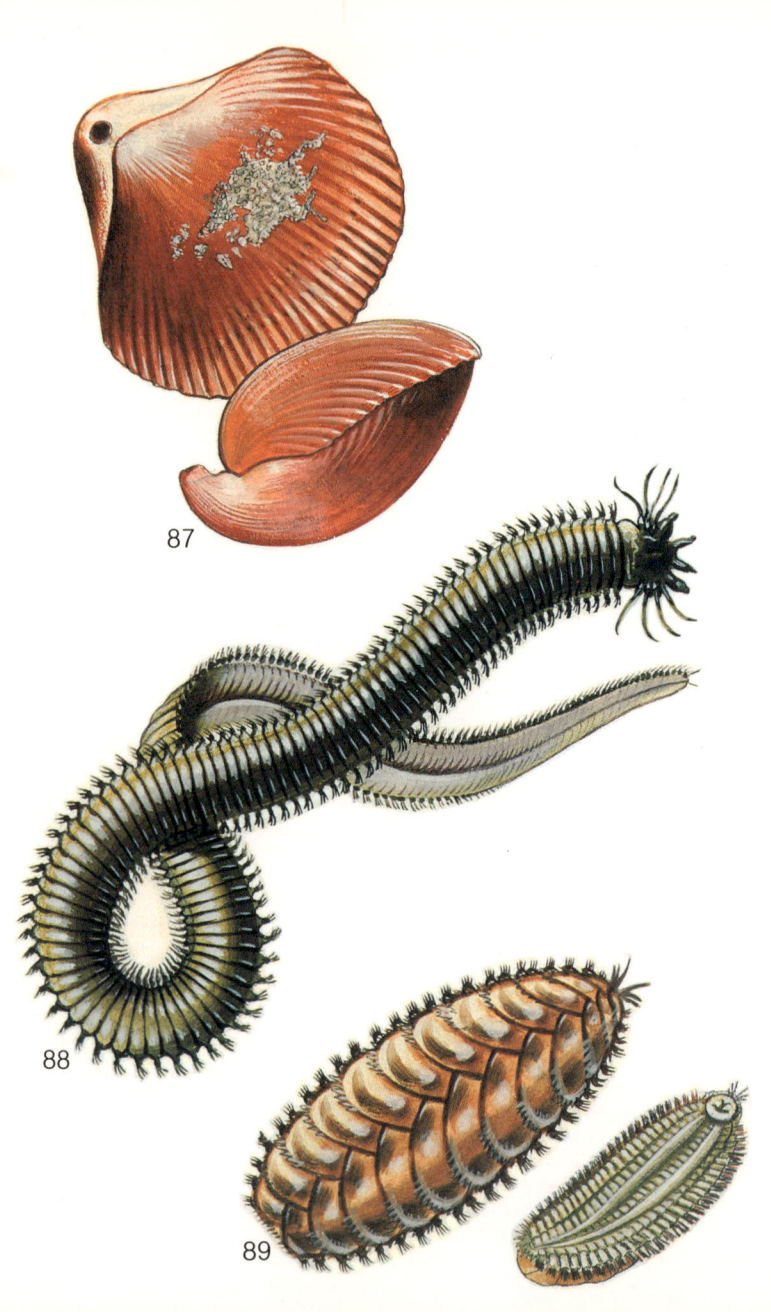

LAMP SHELL

87. **Large red lamp shell** (*Magasella sanguinea*)
Lamp shells look rather like old Roman oil lamps. Although they have two valves, the animal inside differs completely from bivalve shellfish. In life the lamp shells are usually attached to stones, shells or seaweeds by a flexible stalk. We have several lampshells which may be found between tide marks in New Zealand, although most kinds live in deeper water. Altogether there are more lamp shells living here than in most other countries and a number of overseas biologists have made special visits to New Zealand in order to study them.

Although mainly dredged from shallow water from Wellington south, the large red lamp shell is sometimes found under stones at low water.

JOINTED WORMS

88. **Green sea centipede** (*Perinereis novaehollandiae*)
Found throughout New Zealand under stones between tide marks or hidden away amongst mussels, this worm can grow up to 26 cm in length. The group of jointed sea worms is as important in the sea as the related earthworms on land. There are many different kinds but each has a pair of what look like short legs on each segment. When looked at through a powerful magnifying glass it can be seen that these legs or feet are made up of bundles of bristles.

89. **Sea mouse** (*Aphrodite australis*)
This short, oval-shaped, jointed worm represents a group in which the back is protected by a series of overlapping plates. The common name for the group has been given because some species have the back covered by fine hairs. The bunches of bristle feet can be seen clearly on the underside.

Plate 26

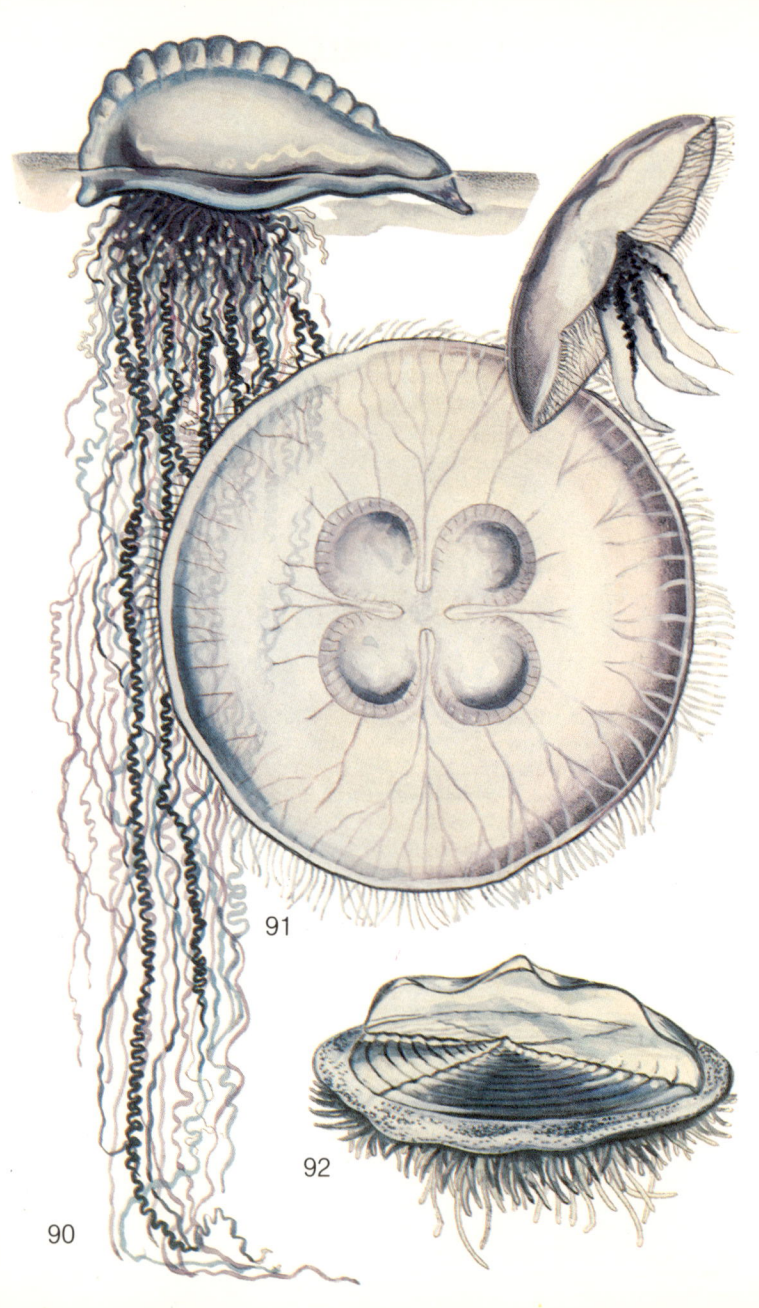

JELLYFISH

90. **Portuguese man-of-war or blue bottle** (*Physalia physalis*)
This is one of the most remarkable of sea creatures, especially adapted for life on the surface of the open sea. A gas-filled float keeps the animal at the surface, while a crest on the float acts as a sail so that the wind can push the man-of-war slowly through the sea. As it moves along, the long tentacles, which can be drawn up and let down like a piece of elastic, cover a considerable area of the sea below. When the tentacles which are armed with stinging cells touch another animal, these cells act automatically. If the catch is small — perhaps a small fish — it will be killed by the stinging poison. The dead prey is then drawn up to the stomach and digested. The men-of-war are commonly washed into shallow waters and onto shore in the summer. The tentacles continue to sting anything which they touch — including swimmers. Large examples in healthy condition may raise long painful welts on human skin. A few people have a more violent reaction to the sting.

91. **Common jellyfish** (*Aurelia aurata*)
Jellyfishes are common in New Zealand waters, especially during summer. The animal consists of a hollow bell and deep saucer. Around the rim of the bell are the tentacles which carry stinging cells. From the centre of the bell a short trunk hangs down with the mouth at the free end. The common jellyfish is almost transparent apart from the deeper coloured, lobed reproductive organs.

92. **By-the-wind sailor** (*Velella velella*)
This is another animal adapted for life on the surface of the open sea. Here the float is a flattened oval shape with a twisted sail mounted on top. Great schools often stretch along our coasts in the summer. Like the man-of-war, the by-the-wind sailor is really a colony of animals, each member of which has become adapted to do one particular job for the colony.

Plate 27

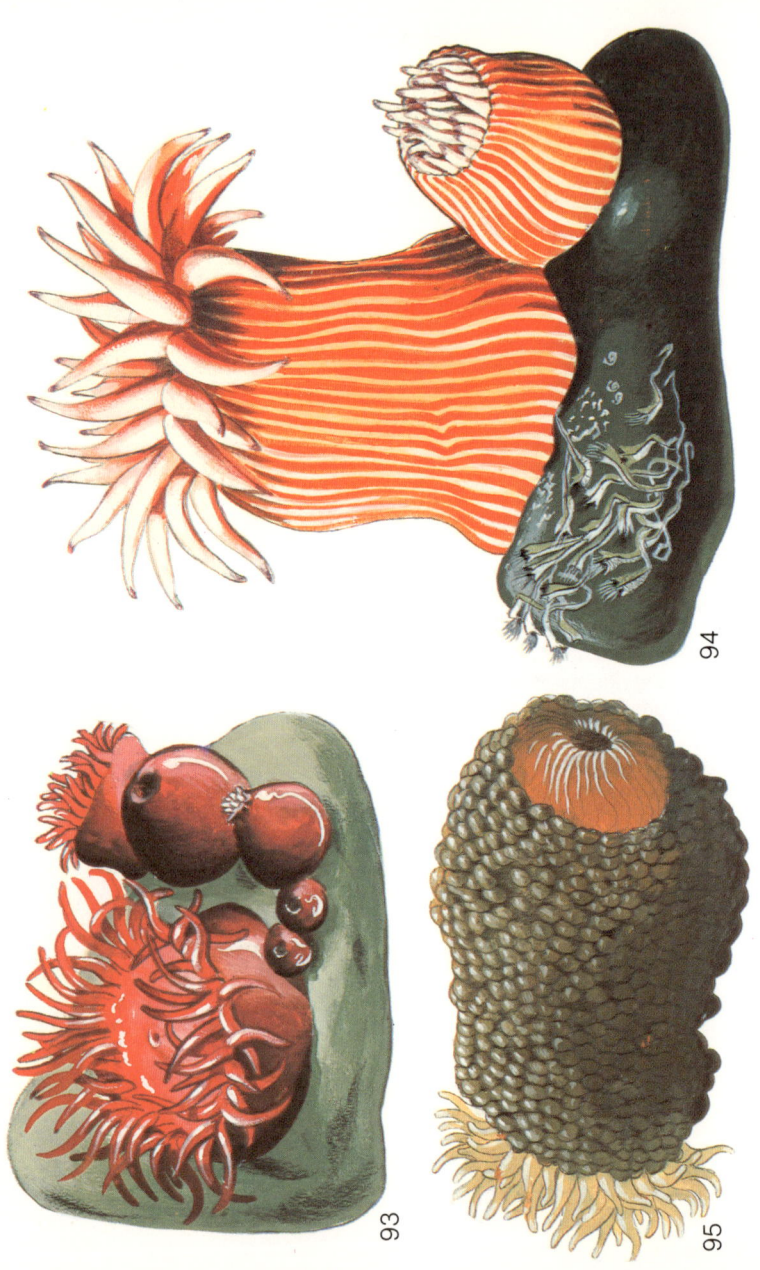

SEA ANEMONES

Sea anemones are related to the polyps which produce corals, but anemones do not produce a skeleton. The tentacles bear stinging cells. Although anemones can reproduce in the usual way by producing eggs and sperm, some can also multiply by splitting in half, while others break up into pieces, each of which grows into a new animal.

93. **Red beadlet** (*Actinia tenebrosa*)
The brilliantly coloured red beadlet is extremely common throughout New Zealand and lives in the open from about half-tide mark upwards. However, it is usually contracted into a large red blob when the tide is out and all too few people recognise it as an anemone. It can be detached easily from smoothish rocks and lives well even in a primitive aquarium, where its appearance when fully open can easily be observed. The eggs develop inside the adult and emerge as fully formed young anemones.

94. **Striped anemone** (*Epiactis thomsoni*)
One of New Zealand's most strikingly coloured anemones, this species is common around Wellington and to the south. It lives in low-tidal pools and just below low-tide mark. This species also broods its young.

95. **Wandering anemone** (*Phlytenactis tuberculosa*)
This is New Zealand's largest anemone — one which grows to over 15 cm. It is usually found loosely attached by the base to seaweeds in rock pools or in the open sea on rocky coasts. It can easily detach itself and move with the waves. When plucked off it contracts at both ends and looks like a warty sea slug. If placed in a jar of sea water, the tentacles will open and the structure of the base can be seen.

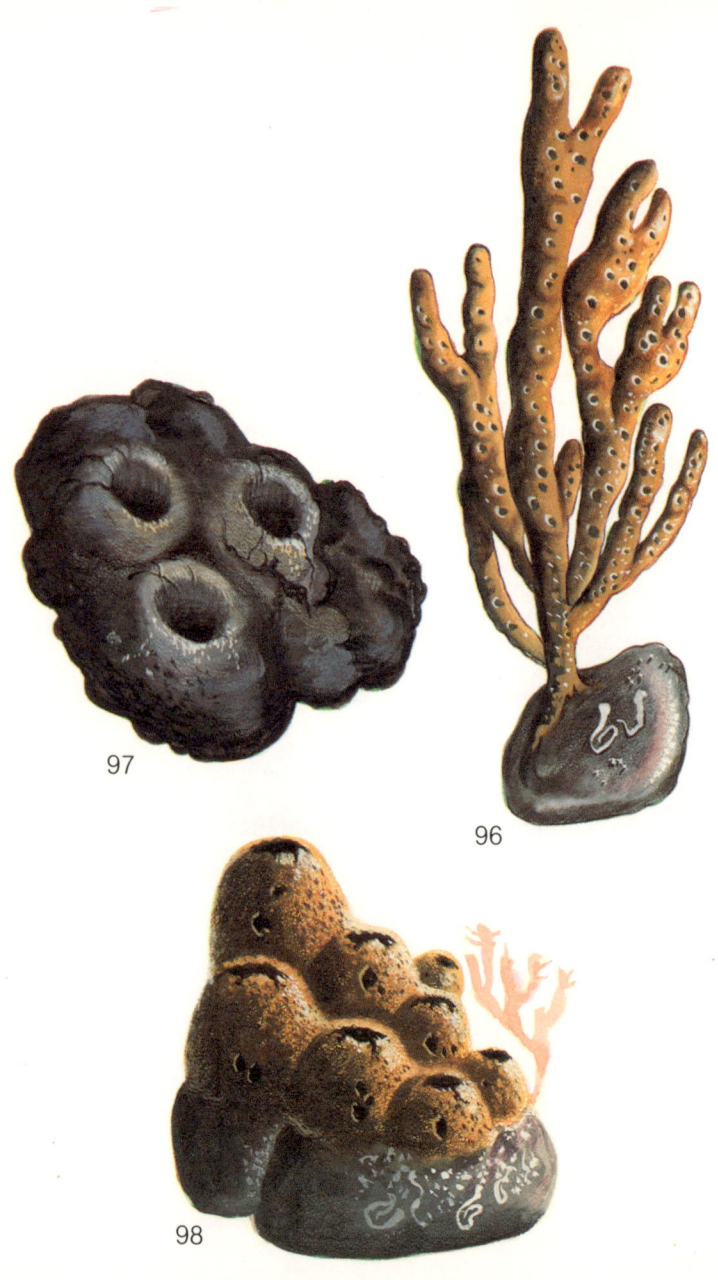

SPONGES

Most people probably feel they can recognise a sponge when they see one. But most sponges in life look rather unlike the soft skeleton of the bath sponge (or its modern plastic equivalent). Few people realise that sponges are really animals. They are primitive colonial animals, made up of cells which do different jobs for the good of the whole colony. Some sponges are simple and small, others clump together or grow into a very large structure indeed.

In life, sea water is drawn in through many small holes, carrying oxygen and food particles. After both are extracted the water passes into a central reservoir and is then passed back to the sea through larger holes. The structure of a simple sponge is shown in Fig. 98. The tiny pores through which water is drawn in and the larger holes through which it passes out can be easily seen.

The living parts of sponges are soft and jelly-like, but the body is stiffened by a skeleton which may be made of flexible material like the bath sponges, or of lime or glassy silica.

96. **Finger sponge** (*Callyspongia ramosa*)
Most often seen when it washes ashore attached to shells or stones. The proportions of the body may be very variable.

97. **Slaty sponge** (*Ancorina alata*)
This dull bluish-grey sponge has a most unpleasant odour when it is washed ashore dead. It is common throughout New Zealand from low water downwards. If a piece is broken off, the tiny, glassy spicules of the skeleton feel prickly.

98. A simple form of sponge with a flexible skeleton.

SEAWEEDS (*Algae*)

Over 600 species of seaweeds live in New Zealand waters and many of them are found on the shore and washed up on beaches. Only a few can be mentioned here. This group of plants can be divided into three sections based on colour: green, brown and red. All really have green colouring pigments but these are masked by other colouring materials in the browns and reds.

In general, greens are found in the highest part of the shoreline, the browns in intermediate areas and the reds deeper down, but there are many exceptions. Seaweeds are as important along the shores as green plants are on land and as diatoms (minute floating plants) are in the open sea. Plants are the only living things that can produce food materials from minerals and gases by using the energy from the sun. In the sea it is the seaweeds and the diatoms that do this work and thus supply the basic food material on which all animal life depends.

99. **Sawtoothed comb weed** (*Marginariella boryana*)
This is a southern form which occurs from Cook Strait south just below low tide. It may grow as long as 2 m. The fronds are long and narrow and have a few teeth along the edge.

100. **Flapjack** (*Carpophyllum maschalocarpum*)
Four species of this group are common in New Zealand. The flapjack occurs throughout the country on open coasts, in sheltered harbours and in tide pools. It often forms a thick band just at low water. The stems and fronds are firm and stiff, with numerous oval, solid floats.

101. **Flexible flapjack** (*Carpophyllum flexuosum*)
This species lives in much the same habitat as the flapjack but in slightly deeper water. It has rounded floats and more flexible fronds which have a slight midrib. The floats in these species help keep the fronds near the surface of the water and thus closer to the sunlight.

SEAWEEDS continued

102. **Bull kelp** (*Durvillea antarctica*)
The giant bull kelp clothes the rock faces of the most exposed, surf-lashed, rocky shores of southern New Zealand with a carpet of writhing, ever-shifting arms. Although more common in the south, it also extends up the west coast of the North Island and to exposed points on the east coast. It has a large, tough holdfast fixed tightly to the rock surface. From this holdfast grow the rounded stalks which expand into wide, heavy blades, which in turn break up to form whip-like thongs. The blades have a thick honeycomb-like layer in the centre, the compartments filled with gas which gives buoyancy. Fronds may grow to 11 m or so in length.

103. **Bladder kelp** (*Macrocystis pyrifera*)
This is the real giant of the seaweed world, New Zealand examples reaching up to 24 m in length. The holdfasts are made up of a complex branching system like the roots of a tree. The illustration shows part of a young example. Plants may grow in quite deep water (down to 18 m or so), and they may form very extensive beds like a marine forest. It is a southern species common from Cook Strait south but loose specimens may float considerable distances.

104. **Paddle weed** (*Ecklonia radiata*)
Although very abundant throughout New Zealand and reaching a length over 2 m, there is no generally accepted common name for this species. It is found just below low water on rocky coasts, often with many plants growing together. There are no floats and the stalk is rounded.

Plate 31

SEAWEEDS continued

105. **Venus necklace** (*Hormosira banksi*)
This is the most common mid-tidal brown seaweed in New Zealand. The thick-walled bladders filled with liquid are well adapted to prevent drying out. It grows on open rock platforms or in rock pools, often with many plants together, in habitats protected from the strongest wave action. The common univalve shellfish, the cat's eye, is often found on this seaweed.

106. **Comb weed** (*Pterocladia lucida*)
This is the only example of a red seaweed given here. Many of these reds are extremely delicate in form and colour and can best be appreciated if they are spread out on a sheet of white paper under water. The comb weed is one of the two local red seaweeds from which agar is produced commercially. It occurs throughout New Zealand but is particularly common along the east coast of the North Island in low-tide pools or just below low-water mark.

107. **Branching velvet weed** (*Codium fragile*)
This green seaweed has a texture very like velvet. It is found throughout New Zealand in pools and on rocks at extreme low water, especially where rocks integrate into sand. The thickness of the cylindrical, branched segments varies considerably.

108. **Sea rimu** (*Caulerpa browni*)
The common name for this seaweed is doubly apt, for its fronds look like the sprays from the rimu tree and the name "rimu" is the general Maori name for seaweed. It is found around low-water mark in the Cook Strait area, but also extends south and as far north as Hawke Bay.

Other books in this series

New Zealand Native Trees I by Nancy M. Adams
Common Birds in New Zealand I — Town, pasture and freshwater birds by Janet Marshall, F. C. Kinsky and C. J. R. Robertson
Common Birds in New Zealand II — Mountain, bush and shore birds by Janet Marshall, F. C. Kinsky and C. J. R. Robertson
Uncommon Birds in New Zealand by Janet Marshall, F. C. Kinsky and C. J. R. Robertson
Freshwater Fish by R. M. McDowall
Mountain Flowers by Nancy M. Adams
Mushrooms and Toadstools by Marie Taylor
Common Ferns and Fern Allies by R. J. Chinnock and Eric Heath
Marine Fishes by John Moreland and Eric Heath
Common Insects by Annette Walker and Eric Heath
New Zealand Native Trees II by Nancy M. Adams